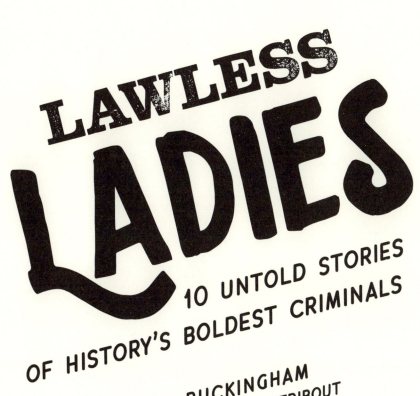

LAWLESS LADIES

10 UNTOLD STORIES OF HISTORY'S BOLDEST CRIMINALS

ANGELA BUCKINGHAM
ILLUSTRATIONS BY RACHEL TRIBOUT

IMPORTANT NOTE
Aboriginal and Torres Strait Islander peoples should be aware that this book contains images and names of deceased persons.

FOR MY MOTHER
— ANGELA

TO AURÉLIE, MAY WE SOON BE
MISCHIEVOUS TOGETHER AGAIN
— RACHEL

Made with love by the team at
FIVE MILE
Alex, Niki, Rocco, Graham, Jacqui, Claire & Lyndal

Five Mile,
the publishing division of Regency Media
www.fivemile.com.au

First published 2022

Text copyright © Angela Buckingham, 2022
Illustrations copyright © Rachel Tribout, 2022
Author photo by Jade Rivére.

All rights reserved. No part of this publication may be reproduced, stored in a retrieval system, or transmitted in any way or by any means, electronic, mechanical photocopying, recording or otherwise, without the prior permission of the publisher.

A catalogue record for this book is available from the National Library of Australia

Printed in China 5 4 3 2 1

THE OUTLAWS

WELCOME	5
OUTLAW MAP	8

Son'ka *the Charming Outlaw*	10
Mary Ann *the Knowing Outlaw*	18
Anne *the Acting Outlaw*	30
Barbara *the Confounding Outlaw*	39
Say Yida al Hurra *the Vengeful Outlaw*	46
Stephanie *the Canny Outlaw*	55
Amy *the Conning Outlaw*	64
Grace *the Negotiating Outlaw*	73
Martina *the Redemptive Outlaw*	80
Cheng I Sao *the Wise Outlaw*	88

Welcome

This is a collection of stories about the most extraordinary, adventurous and daring outlaws I could find. I say 'I could find' because these outlaws may not be the most successful that ever lived. Those particular criminal masterminds are the thieves, pirates and con artists who were never caught. They were so cunning, their crimes were never discovered. But in my search for swash-buckling daredevils I have scoured the stories of our past like a detective to find rulebreakers who were the most ingenious, amusing, wily … and women!

Despite the outrageousness of their adventures, most of the women in these stories are little known. Whether tales of criminals or kings, most of the stories that fill our history books are about men – for the simple reason that for the longest time it was mostly men writing our history. Many women and their stories were simply not included in official accounts. But we need more stories about women who have lived before us in order to better understand our past and ourselves. We need to find the historical clues to put these stories back together.

The ten brazen rule-breakers in this collection prove it was not just men who sailed the seven seas, held up stagecoaches and conned their way into fortunes.

There is another reason why these outlaws' stories were too rarely told: the fearsome prospect of women breaking rules. For centuries, the idea of women as rule-breakers was deeply disturbing, an idea that went against tradition and was, therefore, troublesome. Why? Well, in many cultures, across time, women were seen as being responsible for the raising of children – an important and demanding job. But in societies where that was all women were allowed to do, popular stories reinforced their roles as nurturing, caring people who stayed home and tended the fire. After all, adventures starring women might encourage brave and spirited souls to dream differently …

And yet, we know people dream of all sorts of wild and wonderful things. So it is time to say, "Move over Robin Hood and your band of merry men – we want to hear more about these gutsy girls!"

The outlaws in this book come from all over the world and across time. That is because different societies all over the world have different rules and ways of enforcing them. But wherever there are rules, there are those who will break them.

I have thought about the fact that this is a collection of criminals. Many of these women hurt people they stole from or pirated or tricked. It is also fascinating how many of the women in this collection had very few choices in their lives. These women often suffered the injustices of unequal societies. As females, they were often vulnerable and oppressed. So it is not surprising that they fought back. It doesn't always justify what they did, but may help to explain it. Some of these women's lives as outlaws were bold statements of rebellion against corrupt and exploitative societies.

Other women were just stealing a little gold to get by. Seeking to understand their motivations is a fascinating journey of the imagination.

So while this book is about real stories and research, it is also about imagination – yours, mine, and our shared creative powers. This exploration of defiant women must be inspired by facts but not constrained by them. To properly appreciate the desperate, the dastardly and the devil-may-care anti-heroines of these stories, we must dream about how the world around them looked, smelled and sounded, and how they understood their place in it. So let's be clear, these are adventure stories, not morality tales. These bandits, pirates and con artists fire up my imagination, and I hope they do the same for you.

Enjoy,

Angela

Outlaw Map

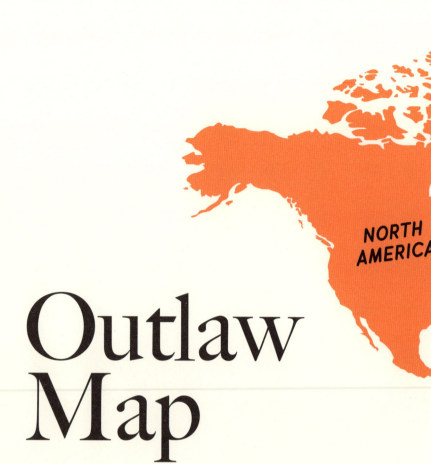

NORTH AMERICA

SOUTH AMERICA

The stories in this collection took place all over the world. The names of regions, countries and towns often change over time. The place names used in these stories are those that would have been known to our outlaws at the time of their stories.

1. Son'ka

2. Mary Ann

3. Anne

4. Barbara

5. Say Yida

LAWLESS LADIES | 8

6.
Stephanie

7.
Amy

8.
Grace

9.
Martina

10.
Cheng

Outlaw Map | 9

Son'ka

THE CHARMING OUTLAW

Nearly 200 hundred years ago, a girl named Sheindlia-Sura Leibovna Solomoniak was born in Warsaw, Poland. Her thieving all over the Russian Empire earned her the nickname – Son'ka the Golden Hand.

Son'ka exhales hard as her maid pulls firmly on the cords of the corset. Each loop is another yank, again and again as Son'ka's waist is roped in. She feels her bust thrust forward and her hips go back as her body contorts.

Son'ka's little monkey squawks in disapproval at the two women.

"Shush little one, I'll be just fine," calms Son'ka in a shallow voice. "Today is an important day so we must dress up."

Son'ka instructs her maid: "I'll wear the silk-satin dress today."

The maid clicks her tongue disapprovingly. "Today, wind is up, season's changing. You'll wear the chiffon."

Son'ka humphs with her hands on her hips as the maid scurries to fetch the petticoats.

"Yes, either," concedes Son'ka. "What I need is to be beautiful and to look very, very rich. Lots of lace and bring out my pearls with the sapphire – something to whet the jeweller's appetite."

Once dressed, Son'ka, her monkey and her maid head to the local market.

The maid chats with the stall holders. "We need a man to pretend to be this young woman's father, so she isn't harassed walking the streets. These are dangerous times. We'll pay well."

A number of old men volunteer loudly.

"Pick me, lovely girl."
"I'll be your papa."
"I'm father to 15 children – I can be your father, too!"

Son'ka's monkey joins the cacophony, screeching her disapproval of the whole scheme.

Son'ka ignores her monkey and the tumble of whiskers, vodka fumes and smelly shirts auditioning to play her father.

She looks around the market stalls. Sitting by a cabbage cart, a little old man smiles as he watches the fuss she has caused.

Son'ka asks him: "Will you be my papa?"

He nods and smiles.

"Will you escort me around town?"

He nods and smiles.

"Do you ever talk?"

The old man just nods and smiles.

> *"I need a gem that will add some sparkle to my dress."*

Son'ka calls to her maid, "I've found him. He is perfect. Now we must take my papa to the barber."

⬆

The jeweller glances up as the bell rings. Coming through his door is a beautiful woman with a monkey! Behind this extraordinary creature is an old but extremely well-dressed man and a simply-dressed woman, who is obviously their servant.

The jeweller has to stop himself from dancing a jig of joy. He can smell the money coming off these people.

"Keep calm, make the sale," he reminds himself.

To these new customers he grins. "Not every day such a beautiful woman comes into my store," he gushes, bowing dramatically.

Son'ka purses her lips modestly. "Please bring a chair for my father."

The jeweller picks up a chair and dashes over to the elderly man, who nods and smiles as he gratefully sits down.

"You're so kind," sighs Son'ka, "and I've come to you for help."

The jeweller is hypnotised by the size of the sapphire on Son'ka's necklace.

Son'ka continues. "You see I have an important evening in two weeks. I will be wearing a cream silk satin and I need a gem that will add some sparkle to my dress."

The jeweller nods enthusiastically. "What sort of gem would

Son'ka: The Charming Outlaw | 13

you like to purchase?"

"Rubies," purrs Son'ka. "I love blood-red rubies."

The jeweller rushes into the back of the shop and soon returns with a tray of red stones.

Son'ka studies them and holds them up to the light. Her monkey sits on her shoulder, watching her inspect the stones.

"Papa, what do you think of this ruby? Would I look pretty in it at Baron Mengden's ball?"

The old man on the chair simply smiles at her and nods.

The jeweller almost chokes. "Baron Mengden? What an honour."

"He's a wonderful friend of my father. Such a lovely man. If he likes my ruby I'll tell him where I got it."

The jeweller beams at the thought of being mentioned in such exalted company.

"But maybe not rubies. Maybe a sapphire would suit me better?" whispers Son'ka in honeyed tones. "They are my favourite gem."

The jeweller races out to get the sapphires.

While he is in the back room, the little monkey leaps off Son'ka's shoulder and onto the bench, picks up two rubies … and deftly swallows them.

LAWLESS LADIES | 14

The jeweller returns with a tray of sapphires.

Son'ka tickles her happy monkey under her chin as she leans forward to look at the blue jewels.

"I might also consider getting some emeralds," giggles Son'ka.

Before the jeweller knows what he is doing, he has trays of every colourful gem – precious amber stones and even diamonds – laid out across the table.

Son'ka flits from tray to tray, asking the jeweller's opinion, and fretting about which will make her look the most beautiful.

While they talk, the cute little monkey runs back and forth, prancing across the table. And when the jeweller's back is turned, the monkey gobbles down one gem here and another there.

Finally, Son'ka decides. She asks the jeweller to wrap up two rubies and a diamond for her.

"Papa, I wish to return to the chateau for a nap. Can you do the rest for me?"

The old man nods and smiles at the beautiful Son'ka.

The jeweller disappears into his back room to prepare Son'ka's parcel of gemstones.

The monkey eats another couple of gems.

Son'ka feeds her a diamond for good measure.

With that Son'ka kisses the old man farewell, puts her monkey up on her shoulder and leaves the store with her maid.

The jeweller returns. The old man is seated, waiting for him.

"Will you pay in gold?" smirks the jeweller.

The old man smiles and nods, as the jeweller packs away the trays of gems.

"I'll just write you up a receipt," says the happy jeweller and he goes to fetch his receipt book from the back room.

The old man smiles and nods. Then he gazes around the empty store. He feels quite uncomfortable that he has somehow been left here alone. The old man gets up, quietly leaving.

The jeweller hears the bell ringing as his door opens and closes, and comes out to find his store empty. Confused and bitterly disappointed, he shakes his head. But it will be days before the jeweller realises his real loss: three rubies, five sapphires, an emerald, a piece of amber and one small and one rather large diamond. Gone.

Back at the hotel, Son'ka takes off her huge hat, her dress and the uncomfortable corset. She sits on her bed in her chemise feeding cherries to her delighted monkey.

"You are such a clever girl," she croons. "Not your everyday circus monkey. Some people run away to the circus, but we ran away from the circus." She kisses the monkey again.

She glances up at the maid. "Get me a sieve from the kitchen."

Later that night, after Son'ka's maid has gone to bed, the lanterns are turned out and the fire burnt down, Son'ka hears the monkey scampering about. She catches her just as her monkey does an explosive poo on the carpet.

"Oh, those cherries did the trick," she whispers.

Taking an old rag, she picks up the poo and dumps it in the sieve. Using the water jug, she washes away the monkey's mess into her own chamber pot. After the watering, nothing but beautiful jewels lie in the bottom of the sieve.

Next morning Son'ka, her maid and monkey hop on a train out of town.

When the police finally catch up with the old man in his fancy morning suit at the market and question him about his beautiful thieving daughter and her monkey, he just smiles and nods.

Son'ka went on to become a queen of crime, running a large gang of thieves and being recognised as one of Russia's most cunning criminals. When she fell in love with a gambler, she pulled off riskier and riskier heists to pay his debts. Finally, she ended up in a Siberian prison. The first time she was jailed she escaped, but was soon captured again.

> **IMPORTANT NOTE**
> *Aboriginal and Torres Strait Islander peoples should be aware that this story contains images and names of deceased persons.*

Mary Ann

THE KNOWING OUTLAW

Almost 200 years ago, Mary Ann Bugg was born the daughter of a newly arrived English convict and a Worimi woman, whose family had been in Australia for millennia. Mary Ann's bush survival skills, her ability to read and write at a time when few could, and her expertise as a spy were crucial to her gang's bushranging successes.

Mary Ann wakes, sensing danger. She looks for the threat around her camp, blue in the cool before dawn. Her beloved Fred – the feared and infamous bushranger Captain Thunderbolt – lies on his swag, gently snoring. He sounds like a big old dog with a cold. Her two little girls, Ellen and Marina, curl into their father, sleeping soundly despite, or maybe because of, his constant rumbling.

Mary Ann casts her eyes to their three accomplices – three bushrangers, fast asleep.

She gets up, stretching her stiff limbs. She rubs the baby in her belly and then checks for danger further away. Her lookout is straight up a gumtree. Usually she can climb with no fuss, but being pregnant, she takes a little longer.

Scanning the horizon, Mary Ann spots a thin trail of smoke in the distance, rising into the morning sky.

LAWLESS LADIES

⬆

The trail of smoke is coming from a campfire. Around that dying fire, five men saddle up their horses.

The police sergeant, a mean, wiry man called Cleary, tells his crew to hustle. "We're hunting bushrangers."

⬆

Mary Ann is back down the tree, fast. "Ellen and Marina, wake up." The children snuggle determinedly under their blankets.

Mary Ann gives Thunderbolt a gentle nudge. "Get up, big man." She calls to the others. "Ya lazy lugs, if you're not up soon the police will be here to serve you breakfast."

The three men jump faster than if she'd poked them with a knife. "What? Where? Who?"

Mary Ann laughs at their confusion. "Smoke's rising from yesterday's camp."

The toughest bushranger, known as Bull, fixes his eye on her. "Our camp?"

Mary Ann nods. "Yep, and they lit a big enough fire that I can see their smoke twenty miles away."

A huge grumpy Scotsman known as Giant mutters, "That means a fair few police are boiling their tea there this morning."

The youngest bushranger, Johnny, whines. "I need a cup of tea."

Mary Ann shakes her head. "If I can spot their fire, they can spot us. Time to go. Have a cracker and get on your horse … if you like living that is."

Thunderbolt packs quickly, loading their loot onto the horses. "You sure it's police?" he whispers.

Mary Ann sighs. "We've been scamping across this country stealing everything that isn't nailed down. It's no shock if they've sent police after us. And to find last night's camp, they must have trackers with them."

Thunderbolt groans. "The police horses are so slow our girls could outrun them, and the squatters are arrogant fools. But those trackers – they find you no matter how fast you ride, how far you go. They see every footprint, every bit of horse dung, every broken stick … "

Mary Ann nods. She already has both children in saddles. Ellen is old enough to ride her own horse. Little Marina sits in front of her mother.

Thunderbolt calls to his men. "Come on pals – the lady says we gotta bolt."

Without another word the crew mounts. The gang gallops away into the bush.

Riding on a dirt road leaves clear hoofprints – it's like hanging up direction signs. To make it more difficult for the police crew to track them, Mary Ann leads her gang into the scrub. She changes their direction often and they ride along the cattle trails and creeks snaking across the land.

⬆

The sergeant and his crew ride in to Mary Ann's morning camp when the sun is high.

The trackers walk carefully around the site. They are of this country, born to families that have been here since before people imagined time. They talk quietly to each other in one of the ancient languages of this land.

"If I can spot their fire, they can spot us. Time to go."

This maddens the sergeant who speaks only English. "What're you two talking about? I don't pay you to chat about things I don't understand."

The two men smile – the sergeant doesn't understand a lot.

One of the trackers graciously explains the current problem. "We got the wrong campsite. There's been kids playing here."

The sergeant shakes his head. "No, that means we got the right place. Thunderbolt must have his brats with him. Great news. They'll slow him down," the sergeant smirks, "Today we'll catch them all."

At every rise in the land, Mary Ann stands in her stirrups, checking for the men chasing them. It is late afternoon when she motions to Thunderbolt, pointing at a distant cloud of dust.

"They're gaining on us," he says and then, with a chuckle, "We could ambush them?"

"Behind a lone tree? With your daughters watching?" Mary Ann scoffs. "No." She passes little Marina to Thunderbolt. "You all get to Birrie River. Hide in the riverbanks."

Mary Ann turns her horse around, then looks back. "And remember, no shoot-outs while you've got the kids."

She gallops back the way they came, toward their pursuers.

Mary Ann stops at a ridge and peers down at the police – five men. She pays particular attention to the two trackers. She guesses they are from Talawanta and are on their own country. Out of respect for their skill she knows she needs a better plan, but for the moment she just plays for time.

She jumps to the ground and rips out clumps of dried grass, wrapping them with small twigs into a bundle surrounded by leather. She pulls out her tinder box, and sparks fly as the flint strikes the metal surface. The bundle catches fire. Now Mary Ann has a flaming torch.

She walks through the surrounding grass, setting it alight. Then she rides back into the wind, sweeping her torch as she goes. It is the end of a hot summer, and the blaze catches quickly, spreading. On and on she rides, trailing fire for nearly twenty miles around her gang's route.

Sergeant Cleary sees the smoke before he sees the fires. "Bloody bushrangers, they're toasting the country."

The trackers agree. "That fire's eating up the clues of where they've gone."

With the rising moon veiled by smoke, Mary Ann heads her horse back towards Birrie River. She finds her family and their accomplices camping on the riverbank as instructed.

The next morning, Mary Ann rises before the sun. She won't get caught sleeping.

Again, she climbs a tree to look across the plains. Her grassfires have burnt out. Dawn reveals long black streaks marking the land. In the opposite direction, she spies hundreds of birds rising and falling. The birds give her hope.

She wakes her crew. "Flocks of birds to the east – could be a lake about forty miles away. That's our best chance to end this game of chase."

On the blackened landscape Sergeant Cleary yells at his men. "We move slower than a funeral procession."

The trackers try to calm him. "We'll keep going. It takes a little time to find the clues in all this ash."

"I want Thunderbolt and his miscreants full of holes," the sergeant growls. "We don't need to waste some judge's time."

⬆

When the bushrangers arrive at the lake, Mary Ann smiles. There are no steep banks, rather the water seeps into the grasslands, hiding tracks. Once in the water, with their hoofprints washed away, she turns to the bushrangers.

"Giant," she orders. "You ride west. Johnny head north, and Bull, you go east for a good long run. Then all of you turn and ride to Collarenebri. Make camp. Thunderbolt will meet you there. They've only got two trackers – they can't go four ways."

As the other bushrangers ride off, Thunderbolt asks, "What about you and the kids?"

Mary Ann laughs. "We're going to keep the coppers here for as long as we can."

Thunderbolt nods and make a promise. "When we lose these police, I'll listen to the bush gossip. I'll come find you – wherever you are."

He kisses his family farewell and rides away to the south.

Mary Ann leads the horses up to the densest growth of trees and ties them up. She sends the girls to collect wood.

Together the two girls and their mother light a big campfire and cook enough dinner for the whole gang.

Mary Ann pulls on a white dress, ties an apron around her pregnant belly and pulls her hair into a simple bun.

Then they wait.

⬆

The sun is slipping down, the lake glowing orange and frogs croaking their evening racket when the trackers spot the girls' footprints. They point towards the cluster of trees.

Sure enough, smoke is rising from a campfire.

Sergeant Cleary jumps off his horse and does a jig of excitement. "Quiet boys. Pull out your guns. We're going to catch us some bushrangers."

Their movement stills the frogs, whose sudden silence sends a message to Mary Ann.

The sergeant creeps up to the site, sneaking from tree trunk to tree trunk.

Mary Ann hears the crack of sticks under heavy boots, the distant whinny of horses that are not her own and the sounds of men hushing each other, all the time stirring her pot of stew.

She gently tells her daughters they are about to have visitors. Ellen, as the big sister, knows what she needs to do and say.

Sergeant Cleary watches the campsite from the trees. It gets darker and darker. The woman feeds the girls, but she doesn't eat herself. She seems to be waiting for someone.

The sergeant finally loses patience and steps out to confront her. "Ma'am, you are the woman of the notorious bushranger, Captain Thunderbolt."

Mary Ann smiles sweetly.

"Where is he?" the sergeant snaps.

"Sorry. I couldn't say," Mary Ann replies.

"When will he be back?"

Mary Ann looks the sergeant straight in the eye. "He's gone to find work. He won't be back for a few days."

Ellen pipes up. "Mummy, that's not right. Daddy said he'd be back tonight."

Little Marina supports her sister. "Remember? He said he'll tuck us in to sleep."

Mary Ann whips around, pretending to be furious with her daughters.

The sergeant sniggers. "Don't mind us, ma'am. We will just wait down by the lake for him."

That night Mary Ann holds both her girls close, whispering in their own language, "I am so proud of you. You tricked that policeman into thinking Dad is coming back. Clever girls."

The next morning Mary Ann has no reason to wake early. She waits till the sun is up and the birds have finished their morning chorus before she leaves her tent. She boils a can of water, gives the girls a good breakfast.

The sergeant storms into camp. She offers him a cup of tea.

He fumes. "My trackers can't find them. Where are your bushrangers?"

Mary Ann just smiles.

The sergeant yells. "Right then. I'm arresting you and your daughters. Stolen property you've got! Vagrancy! The judge will do you for something! It will be a hard ride for four days, but I'm taking you into Bourke if I have to drag you the whole way."

Ignoring the insult, Mary Ann sweetly says, "We can ride."

Mary Ann packs up the camp. As she sets out with her girls, surrounded by the five men, she pretends to be docile. The horses ramble back over the burnt plains. Little Marina squirms in front of Mary Ann, who looks down at her growing belly. It's getting harder to share her saddle. And then she knows exactly what she'll do. She whispers her idea to her girls.

Late in the day Mary Ann cries quietly, with intermittent sobs bursting out.

The sergeant snaps. "What's wrong?"

"Nothing. It is too early." Mary Ann shakes her head. "Maybe the riding is bringing it on."

A short time later she grabs her belly, letting out a roar.

Ellen, with complete authority, turns to the sergeant. "Officer, we have to stop. Mummy is having her baby. Can't have a baby on a horse."

The sergeant pales. "I'm meant to be catching bushrangers – not babies."

Mary Ann huffs and puffs as though holding back the pain. "Just drop us at a cattle station … the closest …" she groans and cries a little more.

The two girls whimper. "Oh Mummy, Mummy, Mummy!"

The sergeant orders the group, "All right, to the nearest homestead!"

To Mary Ann he spits, "This isn't over. We'll send a cart to get you, to bring you before a judge."

Mary Ann is thrilled. It will take the sergeant days to get into Bourke and days for someone else to drive a cart out. With time on her side, she can escape from anywhere.

That evening, a grumpy woman from the homestead kitchen leads Mary Ann and her children inside.

The sergeant commands the stockhands, "Lock up that woman!" And that is the last Mary Ann hears from him.

Two days later, Mary Ann notices the hoot of a night owl at lunchtime. Thunderbolt!

She answers with a whistle.

When Thunderbolt rides up, his family is standing on the verandah ready to go. Before the stockhands understand what's happening, Mary Ann, Thunderbolt and their girls are on horseback, galloping into the distance.

As they ride away, Mary Ann examines the horses. She is impressed. "These are beautiful horses."

Thunderbolt laughs. "I steal only the best for you."

Mary Ann went to the coast to deliver her baby boy while Thunderbolt continued bushranging. Mary Ann later rejoined him, but left the crew when her children needed her to. On one such occasion, while she was away, Thunderbolt was tracked down and killed. Mary Ann Bugg evaded the law, worked as a nurse, purchased land, and lived to an old age.

Anne

THE ACTING OUTLAW

Around 300 years ago, in the Golden Age of Piracy, Anne Bonney sailed the Caribbean. Her daring exploits and panache made her legendary …

Anne strains on her oar, keeping time with her crewmates. Her best friend, Mary, sits across from her. They lean forward as one, dipping their wooden paddles and dragging them through the black water before breaking the surface. Again and again. The longboat powers across the waves.

No sleep tonight. The pirate crew zing with the audacity of their scheme.

Now night is at its darkest. The stars have swung their course. The moon has disappeared, but there is no hint of the coming dawn. This is the perfect time for their crime – the tide is with them.

Their longboat glides into the harbour of New Providence. The pirates slow their paddling to quieten their progress.

Their target towers before them in all her glory. Anne recognises it straightaway, the mighty ship *William*.
They aren't going to pilfer her kegs of rum, treasure or some other loot. No! They are going to steal the whole ship.

Anne chuckles to herself. "It's funny, sailors always refer to their ships as 'she', but then the British Navy gave this ship a boy's name. She is *William*," Anne thinks smiling to herself.

William is the perfect ship for pirates, a sloop with a shallow hull. It can sail through low waters, has British naval cannons on board and plenty of government-issued gunpowder.

The governor recently vowed to catch and kill every pirate in the Caribbean. Anne figures that the governor's job will be a lot harder if pirates have stolen one of the British Navy's own powerful ships.

William is tethered by a heavy line to the end of the pier. It takes skill to manoeuver a ship like this out of harbour.

The longboat glides to a stop under the pier. Anne, Mary and five of their pirate comrades scramble out to climb the wet pylons. Clambering up in the dark, they use the crossbeams to steady themselves.

Anne, carrying a big canvas sack, shimmies up easily. She resembles the men in her trousers and shirt, with her long hair tied back.

Mary is older than Anne, but moves even more quickly. She scaled plenty of masts in her youth as a sailor in the navy. As a skilled climber, no-one had ever guessed she was a woman.

The pirates don't rest on the pier. Instead, like a troop of monkeys, they scamper across the stout line to *William*. Some shimmy across, some swing across – one hand after another. Mary, though, strolls across the rope, as relaxed as a tightrope walker.

Anne is less graceful as she hoicks her body across the rope, lugging her sack with her. Dark red liquid drips, seeping through the canvas of Anne's bag.

The pirates land silently on the ship's deck.

Anne grins as she hears the rumble of snoring. The navy lookout is not looking out, but is sleeping soundly among the ropes, barrels and other equipment. The man's snoring does not surprise Anne. Not one bit.

Earlier in the night, she and Mary had been at a party on this very ship. Wearing their finest dresses, they had encouraged the sailors of *William* to dance and drink plenty of rum.

The still-drunk lookout, soon tied and gagged, wakes to the horror of being captive. With only low light from the ship's brass lantern, he doesn't recognise Anne or Mary in their pirate garb. He grunts and struggles.

Anne swings her sword back and forth before his shocked face. He understands her message, nods and sits obediently while the pirates work.

Mary sits at the top of the ladder that leads below deck to where the rest of the crew sleeps. She cocks two muskets.

Mary is right to be on guard. As the pirates winch up *William*'s massive anchor, the unmistakable cranking of the chain wakes the sleeping navy crew.

Mary laughs quietly as sailors appear at the bottom of the ladder. "Best return to your hammocks, lads, return to your dreams," she tells them. "First time you've heard that order in the navy, but my muskets make this a command you'd better follow."

On deck, Anne directs her fellow pirates. Their biggest challenge is to turn the ship to sail out to the open sea before the navy crew onboard overpowers the pirates or the harbour workers wake. Any alert on shore will lead to the pirates' capture.

The pirates need to have the bow, or the nose, of the ship pointing in the direction they want to go. They search for the kedging anchor, which is the small spare.

When they find this little brother of the main anchor, they ease it down into the longboat waiting at the side of the ship.

Two of the strongest in their team row the longboat with its extra burden further out in the harbour, in the direction they want *William* to turn. They pull away until they have used the entire length of the anchor, then they heave it overboard and signal back to the big ship.

Up on deck, the other pirates put their shoulders to the wooden spokes of a massive winch, the capstan, to wind up the kedging anchor cable and drag the ship around. The crew strains to push the turnstile, but soon *William* nudges away from the pier, her bow slowly turning out to sea.

Anne wants to cheer and shout, but remains silent. Their job is not yet done.

The black night sky lightens to a washed-out blue, and reminds the pirates that the sun is rising. They work faster.

Now comes the most dangerous moment. All pirate hands are needed on deck for the next step to free this ship.

Mary has to leave her position guarding the sailors below. She scuttles up the main mast to release the sails. Two of her fellow pirates work on others.

The glorious white sheets unfurl, catching the first of the golden morning sun. The wind comes in behind them and the sloop surges ahead, out of the harbour.

The dropping of the sails is unmissable. The harbour watchmen come running down the pier, screaming frantically at the pirates as *William* sails away.

At the same moment, the unguarded navy sailors roar up from below deck: shouting, threatening and frantically searching for tools to use as weapons.

Anne, up on the bridge above deck, calmly unties her sack. She removes the axe from her belt.

The navy sailors are rampaging across the deck, vowing revenge, when they hear the crash of the axe.

Above them, up on the bridge, looms a terrifying figure with long wild hair, silhouetted in the dawn light. Anne smashes down her axe, again and again, roaring, while blood splatters all about.

At the sight of this wild, screeching creature, the navy sailors freeze, petrified with fear.

Anne regards them as an actress regards her audience. For at her feet lies an old dressmaker's mannequin in a navy uniform, mixed with a range of offcuts from the local butcher and a bladder of pig's blood. Without a single stab of her sword, gunshot, or even a punch, Anne frightens *William*'s entire navy crew into surrender.

Anne yells to the sailors. "Join us pirates! We steal whatever we want – whatever we need! That damn governor promises he will kill every pirate in these islands, but he hasn't met the likes of us. You can't hang a pirate you can't catch. We control these waters!" She laughs.

The sailors choose whether to become pirates or to stay with the British Navy.

Those who won't join Anne and her crew are lowered overboard to the longboat, which takes them to a nearby beach.

"Join us pirates! We steal whatever we want – whatever we need!"

The thieves and their new recruits sail into the dawn – aboard the newest pirate vessel in the Caribbean.

Anne Bonney and her fellow pirates sailed the waters of the Caribbean, plundering as many as nine boats in the next two months in their fine ship. But the audacious theft of William *made the humiliated governor determined to catch them. A British Navy vessel tracked down the ship and the pirates were defeated. The men were all speedily executed, to which Anne made the famous remark: "If you had fought like men, you would not have died like dogs." Anne and Mary escaped execution because they claimed to be pregnant. Mary died in prison, but Anne escaped to continue her adventures.*

Barbara

THE CONFOUNDING OUTLAW

Nearly 300 years ago in a small medieval town, near the border of Liechtenstein, Barbara Erni was born to homeless parents. Determined not to remain poor, she travelled all over Western Europe thieving.

Barbara raps on the roof of the carriage, but the wheels keep rolling. A boy sleeps with his head on her lap.

Another passenger, a gentleman with whom she has been speaking, is much more forceful.

He knocks hard on the carriage roof, opens the window and calls out to the driver. "Stop this carriage. The lady is tired, her boy is exhausted, and they wish to stop at the inn."

The carriage rolls to a halt.

The gentleman and the driver easily lift Barbara's trunk off the back of the carriage. "Let us carry your trunk to the inn door," they offer.

But Barbara frets. "I have held you up too long already," she says. "Please continue your journey. I will ask the host of the inn to help me from here. My trunk is not heavy, and you have already been too kind."

The driver and other passengers farewell the lady.

The gentleman passenger bows his goodbye, thinking: "How lovely she is. What extraordinary golden hair."

He has not yet noticed that he is lighter of his purse.

As the carriage disappears over the rise of the road, Barbara puts her arm around the boy's shoulders. "Are you ready to do this?"

The boy flashes a mischievous grin. "I'm always ready."

They share a long hug.

Barbara walks up the path to the inn. When she knocks on the front door of the inn, the boy is gone.

The innkeeper, a large, dour man, opens the door.

Without a smile, he acknowledges his gracious visitor. It is unusual to see such a woman with such blonde hair. It is more unusual to see a woman this tall. It is even more unusual to see a woman so finely dressed in this part of the mountains. The inn get lots of travellers, merchants, tradesmen, but not many fine ladies.

The innkeeper's dogs bark at her.

Barbara is completely unfazed. She entreats the innkeeper. "Good sir, I need your help – a room for the night. My trunk is just down here," she points a little way down the path, "and I cannot lift it alone."

"Right, come inside," he instructs. "I'll send some of the lads out to pick up your trunk."

"So kind, but I dare not leave it," she says apologetically. "I'll just sit and wait with my trunk until your men can help me bring it inside."

The innkeeper's wife joins her husband at the door.

Barbara skips down the stairs and sits gracefully on her wooden trunk. It is engraved, the pretty patterns hiding the small holes in the woodwork.

Barbara gazes up at the charming inn, with its pretty green shutters and the walls freshly painted. Many pots of red and white flowers contrast beautifully with the glorious green hills behind the chalet. Beyond the hills, mountains rise up to rocky peaks topped with white snow. This is a prosperous inn.

She gently knocks on the trunk three times. Two quiet knocks respond from inside. Their scheme is underway.

Up at the inn door, unaware of the knocking below, the innkeeper and his wife watch Barbara.

"What's a woman like that doing travelling on her own?" wonders the innkeeper's wife.

"Well, she's right nervous about her trunk," grumbles her husband. "Won't be parted from it."

"She looks rich," says his wife.

"That she does," agrees the innkeeper.

"I say we be especially nice to her, offer her the goose and dumplings with red cabbage for dinner and charge her double," chuckles the innkeeper's wife.

"Have you ever been robbed ...? Where is the safest place in your fine establishment?"

Barbara: The Confounding Outlaw | 41

As the innkeeper and Barbara watch the young men lug the heavy trunk into the inn, Barbara complicates things.

"Will my trunk be safe in my room?" she asks, anxiously. "Have you ever been robbed before? Where is the safest place in your fine establishment?"

The innkeeper assures her, "The safest room is the cellar."

She shakes her head skeptically, "Now, I do not want to be rude, but we are not just putting my family treasure … "

She slaps her hand over her mouth. "I didn't mean to say that. I meant … er, my trunk. I'm not just putting my trunk way down in the cellar. My trunk needs to be safe. The safest place in your inn."

The innkeeper hushes this nervous, ditzy and wealthy woman, and holds up his finger.

He directs the young men to leave the trunk in the dining room.

When everyone else has left the hall, the innkeeper leads Barbara to the dining room. There is dark green panelling running right around the room, only broken by the fireplace.

Barbara sniffs. "Here? This doesn't seem safe to me. Everyone comes in and out of here. This is probably the busiest room in your whole inn."

The innkeeper finally grins at her as he reveals his clever secret. He unclicks one panel, which swings open to reveal a little keyhole. He unlocks the secret door, opening a hidden cupboard.

Barbara peers in, sees bags of gold, silver candlesticks and a few dusty bottles of wine.

She turns back to the innkeeper. "Well, that is clever!" she compliments him. "And I presume only you have the key."

The innkeeper brags, "No-one can get in there but me."

Barbara inspects the lock on the inside of the secret door closely. "I see how this lock works," she exclaims. "Yes, the key just moves this little lever, and when the lever is down nobody can get in. When the key turns in the lock, the lever pops up and your secret door opens. Very clever. Yes, this will do nicely. You are too kind," she gushes.

The innkeeper marvels at Barbara's strength as they push the trunk themselves, sliding it into the secret chamber. Neither of them want the rest of the house knowing where the treasure is hidden.

"Thank you so much," sighs Barbara. "Now I feel safe."

Barbara gives him a gold coin from the silk purse she pickpocketed in the carriage.

The innkeeper grasps the gold coin, but pretending to be polite declares, "You don't need to pay me now. We can sort it all out when we settle the bill."

"No," charms Barbara. "It is not for the accommodation or dinner or breakfast, but for looking after me and my trunk."

Inside the secret chamber, the boy listens. He waits for quiet, then pushes up the lid of the trunk. He climbs out. In the dark he eats his bread and cheese, drinks from his water bottle, and waits.

That night, Barbara eats the roasted goose in the dining room. The innkeeper and his wife can't believe that she accepts the outlandish price they charge. Both hope she will stay for a few days and they can extract much more gold from her.

No-one notices when, instead of eating her dessert, Barbara wraps the cake in a serving cloth and pops it in her purse.

Barbara bids everyone goodnight, adding, "I am exhausted! There is no need to wake me in the morning. I will stay a few days. The food is so good. The inn so comfortable. I will rest here until I feel strong enough to travel again."

When the inn is completely silent, the boy takes out his flint box and lights a candle.

He searches for the lever he heard Barbara describe. Sure enough – here it is. His little hands have no problem flicking the lever. From the inside, unlocking the secret cupboard is easy.

As the little door opens into the dark dining room, he sees the white teeth of Barbara's smile.

Together, they silently load the innkeeper's treasures into their trunk, making sure the gold coins don't jingle and the silver candle sticks don't clank as they are packed away.

The boy steps out of the cupboard. They blow out the candle, so no-one sees their light. Barbara gives the boy a light kiss on his cheek and passes him the cake from her dessert. Then she lifts the heavy trunk up on to her back. She and her little accomplice sneak out of the chalet, climbing up the mountainside away from the inn.

The next morning, nobody knocks on the door of the gracious traveller.

When the midday meal passes and Barbara has not stirred, a maid is sent to check on her. The maid steps into the darkened room and sees a sleeping body in the bed. She creeps away quietly, afraid to wake such a wealthy guest.

It is not until dinner passes that the innkeeper's wife checks the room. She howls when she finds the sleeping body is just an arrangement of pillows with the blankets pulled over them, and a sleeping bonnet artfully arranged.

By then Barbara and her boy are long gone.

Barbara Erni's daring thefts made her rich and a legend in Liechtenstein, but her fame led to her downfall. She was caught, confessed to 17 burglaries and was the last person in the country to be hanged. She protected the identity of her accomplice by never revealing his name. He was never caught.

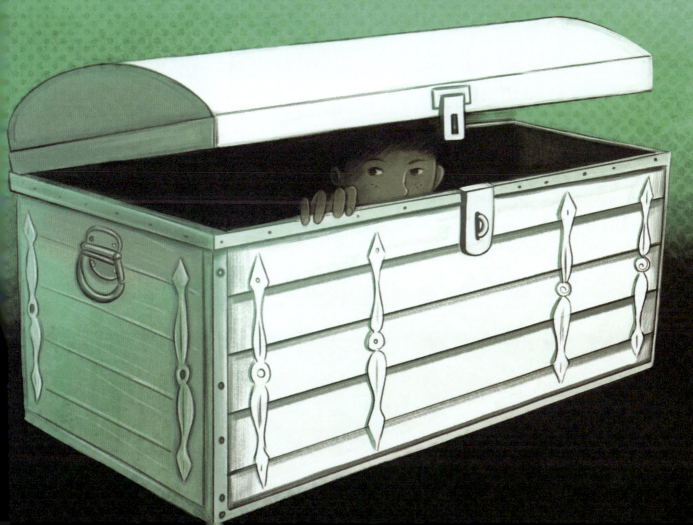

Say Yida al Hurra

THE VENGEFUL OUTLAW

About 500 years ago, Queen Isabella expelled all non-Christians from Spain. This caused floods of people to go elsewhere in search of new homes. Among them was a child, Say Yida al Hurra, whose family finally settled in the north African fort city of Tétouan on the Mediterranean Sea. From here she became a pirate queen, providing her harbour as a refuge for the Barbary pirates who plundered the Mediterranean.

Say Yida al Hurra counts the wretches shuffling down the gangplanks from the huge pirate boats. They all look scared and tired, but the first group of people coming off the ships is kept well apart by the pirates.

These families now stand waiting on the pier. They claim al Hurra's attention because they remind her of her own family arriving here. In this terrified cluster she watches the parents with their children peeking out from around their legs. Small faces peek up at her busy port, at the white houses built on the gentle hill to her fort and, behind all this, up to the mountains that ring her town, now illuminated by the sun rising from the sea.

Say Yida al Hurra points down at the group of families, ordering two pirates, "Bring them up to my fort. Make sure they are fed, given water, let them wash. Welcome them."

There is no such reception for the other people herded off the boats onto the pier. Say Yida al Hurra marches toward this cowering crowd. These people are not her people. They are not of her religion.

The golden charms lining Say Yida al Hurra's silk head scarf jingle as she advances. Behind her rushes her secretary. The young man takes notes. There is much work to be done. Sixteen huge galley ships crowd into port.

Pirates and port workers rush up and down gangways unloading treasure – bags of gold, fine silver plates, weapons and anything else the pirates were able to carry off during their attack on Gibraltar.

The unloading is directed by Oruç, the most fearsome of the pirates, with a long red beard. His silk vest and fine turban can't hide that he is a man used to hard labour and a tough life at sea. At his waist hangs a shining, curved sword. He points to where the cargo must go. The sun glints off his silver hand, which replaces the real one lost in a battle long ago.

Oruç hears Say Yida al Hurra walking up behind him. He turns, bows low.

"You've done brilliantly," she congratulates him. "It takes a lot of gold to maintain my fleet of ships, a lot of gold to protect our town, a lot of gold to save our people. And you have brought me a lot of gold."

The gruff pirate smiles as he bows again before her.

Say Yida al Hurra continues. "Now we must focus on our captives. They might be the most valuable treasure you have brought me."

Confused captives still trail off the ships, nervously inching down the gangplanks, wobbly on legs used to the rocking of the ships, blinking in the sun after being held below deck.

Say Yida al Hurra questions Oruç. "Exactly how many people have been taken captive?"

Kidnapping is only the beginning of this enterprise.
She lines the captives into six groups of ten on the pier.

In Spanish she announces: "Every one of you is now my prisoner. I will first tell you the good news – it is not in my interest to kill you because I need you alive for ransom. We will negotiate with your families and your priests. We will fix a price and they will buy you back. It is not in my interest to starve or mistreat you. I want to send you home healthy. I don't want you. I want your gold. I am the most trusted negotiator in the Mediterranean because I keep my word, which is why your people will pay the price I ask."

Many of the captives sigh with relief, but al Hurra continues, "The bad news is – there are a lot of you. If you are a problem for me, I will make sure you are not a problem. Understand, I do not feed problems."

The captives nod in understanding. They watch Say Yida al Hurra as she strides up and down through the lines of prisoners, proclaiming her orders. She does not shout but her voice is even, firm and commanding.

> "Every one of you is now my prisoner ... the good news ... I need you alive for ransom."

"Now to start this process, I need your name and place of birth. For those of you who come from noble families, you will pay the largest ransom. And don't think you can trick me to avoid it. Your family back home won't pay unless they are confident they are getting the family member they have lost – you. If you think you can pretend to come from a poorer family, if you try to cheat me out of the ransom, or think you can get home on the cheap, you will confuse the matter. Confusion is bad for negotiation, and your lives depend on this negotiation going well. Understand?"

One at a time each captive mutters their name. The secretary notes their details. With so many prisoners the process takes time. The sun climbs higher in the sky.

Al Hurra does not rush. She studies each person intently. She reaches out and feels along the seams of one man's vest. Her fingers run down the fabric. She feels something and jerks the vest off the man. She rips at the seam. It holds fast. She holds the material between her teeth and tears. Into her hands fall two sparkling blue gems and two gold coins.

"How did you know?" stammers the man.

"I know everything," growls Say Yida al Hurra. But she whispers to her secretary, "The clothes of every captive must be checked, even women's petticoats."

She continues pacing the queues. She interrogates faces, checks teeth, hands and twists heads around to inspect earlobes.

"What are you searching for?" asks her secretary.

"Clues of wealth. How healthy is the human before me? Have they thrown off an earring showing that they come from a wealthy family? What rings have they pulled off their fingers to hide from me?"

The sea winds rustle the fine silk of Say Yida al Hurra's gown. She continues. "The trick in any negotiation is knowing how much you can ask for. I can't ask for money people don't have when negotiating a ransom. No point asking a poor village for a king's ransom. But it would be a tragedy to capture a king and ask for a ransom that could be paid by one poor village.

"Have you ever caught a king?" asks the awestruck secretary.

"Not yet," laughs Say Yida al Hurra. "But I've had a fair few lords end up here in my port."

At the end of the last line, a young woman mutters her name and place of birth. "I was born in Granada," she whispers.

The secretary writes it down.

Say Yida al Hurra is hooked. "I was born in Granada too, the most beautiful town, on the hill, fountains, water running through the city, gardens, the orange groves. I still remember standing on the walls of the Alhambra and looking out to the snowcapped mountains, far, far away."

"It is the most beautiful town," agrees the young woman, eagerly. "When I married I had to leave. Two years ago."

"I was banished more than twenty years ago," snaps Say Yida al Hurra, her childhood memories blown away by visions of how she left. "And if in the next few weeks you ever wonder how you came to be captured by my pirates – you can thank the Spanish queen who sent soldiers to kill my people, forced my father from his home, taking only what he could carry while my mother held my hand and we ran for our lives."

The young woman fearfully questions Say Yida al Hurra. "What will you do if our families won't pay the ransom?"

The woman's plea ends al Hurra's anger. "I will not kill you," she calmly states. "Have no fear."

With that, her list of captives is complete. "Take these captives down to the dungeons!" she commands. The lines of prisoners are marched away from the port, the sea and the sun, into the cool darkness of the caves below the city, where they will await their fate. Rough rock will hold them until the gold arrives to buy their freedom.

Say Yida al Hurra and her trusted pirate, Oruç, walk back up to her fort. He questions her, "That was not truthful – when the young woman asked you what will happen if her ransom is not paid. You said you will not kill her."

"I won't kill her," agrees al Hurra.

"But you sell as slaves anyone whose ransom is not paid."

Say Yida al Hurra keeps walking. "Truthful? From a pirate? We can't tell them what will happen. Fear makes people unruly. It is hard to control scared people. They are not our people. The truth is this: on this voyage you stole a lot of gold and you saved a lot of refugees, a lot of our people."

Oruç presses on. "Their people, our people – this is about more than gold, more than my simple piracy. This is about revenge. Revenge for what happened to your family."

Al Hurra ignores his last comment. "We must hurry to care for our new arrivals."

In her fort, in a large, tiled room, with white arches leading out to a courtyard garden, Say Yida al Hurra welcomes the families who were the first to disembark from the boats. Now the children play in the fountains and under the orange trees.

There is a system for the new arrivals. For each family she makes a note of their names, places of birth, skills and trades.

Say Yida al Hurra generously promises, "You will live in the town. We have houses where you can stay until you can build your own home. You are safe. You will be welcome here." She gives them gold and food to start a new life.

One old man weeps before her – he has lost his farm. "I carry the keys to my old home. I locked the door as the soldiers came. Now I have my keys, but no home. I was born on that land, my sons were born there, my grandchildren. And now we have been chased away, washed up on your shore, forced to live off your charity."

Say Yida al Hurra comforts him. "I still have the keys to my father's house. When my father washed up on this shore there was nothing, just the rubble of an old fort destroyed by the Spanish. See what we have built. We built the fort, we built homes, we have farms – and one day we will go home."

Say Yida al Hurra continued her piracy and kidnapping operations. She continued to take in refugees. She ruled Tétouan as governor for nearly thirty years but neither she nor her people ever returned home to Granada.

Stephanie

THE CANNY OUTLAW

One hundred years ago, Stephanie St Clair, an immigrant from the French West Indies, rose to control one of the most successful underground gambling rings in New York City, living and working in Harlem. When times became tougher with the Great Depression and the end of Prohibition, the criminal big shots tried to take over her racket...

Stephanie St Clair smashes her silver-topped walking stick through the glass cabinet. The shining shards splinter across wrapped parcels of butter and cheese.

The storekeeper retreats behind an aisle of cans.

Two huge men lumber out of the storeroom at the sound of the smash.

To their shock Stephanie comes straight for them. She pushes past their massive forms, storming into the back room. Here she grabs the betting slips organised across the table.

"What are you two boys doing working for Dutch Schultz?" she interrogates, as the young men try to stop her messing up their betting system.

One of the men laments, "I have to pay rent, Madame St. Clair. I do what I must to get by. We're not your problem. We just work for Schultz."

"Too right," agrees Stephanie. "Where is that coward? He pays people to try and kill me, but he hides away like a mouse. If he wants a slice of my numbers game he should come take it himself, not send snivelling traitors to try and take me out."

"He's not hiding from you, Madame. He's hiding from the tax man."

"You pass up the chain that he should be hiding from me, because I won't pay no white man. Even if he's the most murderous, mean white man around. I won't pay him the profits from my numbers game."

Stephanie lights a match and drops it onto the pile of betting slips. As the smoke rises, she turns, her fur coat swishing around her.

Gliding out the door she calls back at the storekeeper: "You need to choose your friends better. When you stop working for Dutch Schultz, come and see me. Maybe I'll help you clean up this mess."

It is a busy day for Stephanie. She swings past each of Schultz's game rooms, repeating her threat that Schultz should come after her himself.

After a long day of confrontations, she heads back to her own betting rooms, which are busier than any bank in New York City. She nods to her staff, the controllers and the office secretaries tabulating the bets. Runners wait in line to hand in the bets they've collected through the day.

Stephanie employs forty runners, who go through her neighbourhood, Harlem, collecting people's bets in her numbers game. She takes penny bets. This is a game designed for poor people who can't afford putting money on the horse races.

An ever-present, deep-seated cruelty keeps Stephanie's neighbourhood poor. There are spoken and unspoken rules restricting where people can live, work and shop, and how they do just about anything, according to the colour of their skin.

For years, none of the mob – the big-time criminals who were all white – could be bothered with Harlem's number games. They assumed the small bets of this poor community didn't make much money. But with the Depression hitting, getting work is hard, earning money is hard and times are tough for everyone. Even the criminals. Now white mobsters like Dutch Schultz want to cash in on black Harlem's numbers game – Stephanie St Clair's numbers game.

Mr Brown walks into her betting rooms – Stephanie's favourite runner. He's always well dressed with pants perfectly creased, shoes shined and wearing a well-cut jacket.

Stephanie respects him because he doesn't carry betting slips. Instead, he writes the numbers in the newspaper he always carries under his arm. In all the years he's been running numbers for her, he's never been caught by the law.

If all her runners were as effective as Mr Brown, she wouldn't have to pay large bribes to the local police.

Mr Brown tips his hat to his boss.

"What's happening out there, Mr Brown?" Stephanie asks.

"Where is that coward? ... If he wants a slice of my numbers game he should come take it himself."

Stephanie: The Canny Outlaw | 57

"Busier than ever ma'am. Plenty of five-cent bets for three numbers in a row and even more two- and three-cent bets for the combination of numbers. We've done well today, like every day, Madame St Clair."

Stephanie thinks a moment. "Anyone stepping on your route? Any thugs knocking at doors?"

"Couple of Dutch Schultz's young lads have been asking around today. Yeah, they're knocking on doors. The competition's always sniffing around, trying to take our customers, wanting to set up in our buildings."

Stephanie rolls her eyes in annoyance.

"Don't worry, Madame. People know you play fair. You don't rig the numbers and you pay them out when they win," continues Mr Brown.

"But our competition is getting rough. People won't play if they are scared," worries Stephanie.

"You've been paying for nearly ten years and that wins you loyalty from your customers. You've covered their rent in tough times, run a fair insurance scheme, paid for funerals, paid for street parties, paid in to the charities. If they bet with anyone – our people will bet with you," suggests Mr Brown.

Bumpy Johnson barrels through the door, interrupting the conversation.

Loud, young and full of laughter, Bumpy chortles. "Excuse me, Madame St Clair, how am I meant to protect you when you go all over town, on your own, telling Dutch Schultz to find his bravery button and come after you himself?"

The young man chuckles as he flings his hat on to the hat stand. "Ma'am I've been chasing you from one betting room to another, finding nothing but crying men and broken glass."

Stephanie laughs. "Dutch Schultz even offered Caroline Odlum $500 to kill me. Caroline can't bake a cake, let alone kill anyone. For five years he has been trying to take over our game. I've had it with him. I don't hurt anybody, let alone kill them. I'm just running the numbers! Dutch Schultz is worse than indigestion. If he didn't have the police on his side, the politicians in his pay, we would have run him out of Harlem."

Bumpy shakes his head. "You gotta take this seriously, ma'am. He's killed people trying to get to you. He even killed a member of his own crew – at dinner! He's a nasty, nasty man."

"I do take this seriously – like the plague," Stephanie shoots back. "But me work for Dutch Schultz? Run Dutch Schultz's game for him? That is not going to happen."

With that, Stephanie goes home, driven by limousine to her apartment.

She lives on Sugar Hill, an area of Harlem filled with artists, lawyers, academics and writers. She fits right in, as a champion for her community, always elegant and speaking exquisite French.

The concierge opens the door for her. The elevator operator takes her up to her apartment.

Stephanie's in her bedroom, dressing up for an evening out, when she hears a knock at the door.

"Ah, Bumpy," she exclaims. "I told you I'm okay."

She swings open her front door. A squat man, with his hat pulled low, points his gun at her.

"Please come in," she says politely.

As the gunman walks through her front door, she trips him with her walking stick.

He drops the gun. She pushes his back, swings open her coat wardrobe, gives him another shove and slams the cupboard shut behind him.

Bumpy is still in the office when the phone rings.

"Hello, Bumpy."

"Yes, Madame St Clair."

"Bumpy, I have an unknown man in my coat cupboard. I'm worried about my fur coats. He doesn't look like the sort to appreciate style."

Five minutes later, Stephanie checks out her window.

Her long, black limousine is pulling back up outside her apartment block. Her team jumps out in their suits. They come up to her flat and escort the meddlesome man away.

Bumpy remains in her living room.

"Okay, Bumpy," Stephanie tells him. "You are right. It is time to act."

Madame St. Clair heads back to her bedroom and changes into a long, sparkling evening gown in a magnificent peach colour. She rolls on long white gloves and wraps a fancy fur trim around her shoulders.

Her limousine carries her to the favourite club of the local police commander.

As the car door is opened for Stephanie, Bumpy is nervous.

"Do you think this is going to work?" he asks her. "You've asked the police for help and they've done nothing. Everyone knows Dutch is out to kill you. He advertises the fact. The police haven't done a thing."

Stephanie just keeps walking. The doorman coughs as Stephanie and Bumpy swish past, but the maître'd knows this pair.

"We're here to see the commander," Stephanie charms.

They are led through the all-white audience to a table with a corpulent man smoking a cigar.

Stephanie sits down before being invited. Bumpy stands behind her as a large reminder no-one is to touch her. "Commander, I am going to give you some valuable information," Stephanie announces and then pauses for effect. "The whereabouts of Dutch Schultz's main betting office. Now, I know Dutch isn't there because the man is a chicken."

"A murderous chicken," agrees the police commander. "But I don't know that we want to be disrupting things in Harlem. Could cause a lot of blood to be spilt."

"There is already a lot of blood being spilt," states Stephanie. "So you need to bust up his betting offices and shut down his Harlem operation."

"Now why would I do that? Why would I attack Dutch Schultz?" the commander smirks.

"I wouldn't be here chatting with you if I didn't understand your situation," states Stephanie, staring back at the commander. "I know Dutch Schultz has paid the police much more than I ever have, given the size of his operations, but you will do what I ask because … Well," Stephanie pauses and then presses on, "because there is a commission underway into police corruption."

The commander's eyebrows rise and his face grows pale.

"Yes, indeed," she says, nodding. "I know all about it. Apparently your political masters are upset that you police take so many bribes. They want to stop you getting a second pay cheque. I am going to go to the anti-corruption commission and tell them the name of every police officer I've bribed, with receipts and a notebook of who I paid what when. You and I both know that the commission will not send me to jail. Those judges will forgive my crimes if I am revealing crimes by the police … but I won't mention your name or any of your team if you take my tip on Dutch Schultz."

Ash from commander's cigar drops, burning a hole in his trousers. Still his mouth hangs open.

Stephanie smiles at him.

The police commander gulps down his drink and then splutters. "You won't go to the commission. You'll blow up your business. No police officer will ever trust you again. Without police protection, you have no business. You know the system. You wouldn't dare speak to the commission."

Stephanie shakes her head. "The system is rotten. I won't work for Schultz. So I'm out. I'm not greedy. I've made enough money. You could say I'm retiring. Going straight. No more bribing police. No more numbers game. The only question is, do I mention our friendship to those judges? I'm going to appear next week. Your choice."

Stephanie stands, twirls her walking stick and leaves the bar.

On the way out, she sniffs: "I wouldn't drink here anyway."

The police moved against Dutch Schultz, confiscating $12 million from his offices and arresting fourteen of his gambling staff. Stephanie went to the anti-corruption commission and testified against crooked police. Stephanie handed her gang over to Bumpy Johnson. Her life continued eventfully. She served ten years in prison for attempting to murder her lover, but Dutch Schultz never got her. He was killed by gangland associates.

Amy

THE CONNING OUTLAW

Just over 100 years ago, Amy Bock was an experienced con artist who scammed people across New Zealand. Over time, the police became aware of her exploits, so she had to radically change her appearance.

Amy tightens the white bow tie under her shirt collar. She looks at herself in the mirror: "No-one can make me embroider, tidy house or cook their dinner. I will not promise to be an obedient, dutiful wife. No, not me – for I am a handsome, dashing fellow."

True, she is small for a man, but she has a strong jaw, her short hair has a nice wave and the grey streaks make her seem trustworthy.

She chortles. "A handsome chap indeed! Makes me wish I was Percy Redwood. Such a decent bloke."

Furious knocking on the door interrupts Amy's self-assessment. The door flings open. Her bride to be, Nessie, storms into the room, a whirlwind of lace and tears. Her face is wet, her nose snotty, her long white dress unbuttoned and her brown hair wild.

"Percy, I've just heard the most terrible thing," Nessie wails.

LAWLESS LADIES | 64

"Three men came to the house last night, all saying you owe them money, a lot of money! Mama had to pledge our home as surety you would pay the money back!"

Amy beams. "Why, my love, that's not a terrible story. It is a wonderful story. It shows your mother has faith in me."

Nessie is confused, but Amy continues in soothing tones. "She understands my troubles. Now, if my mother had arrived as planned, and brought with her my monthly allowance, a very generous sum of money, mind you, none of this would have happened and you would have nothing to cry about. But then I would never have known just how much your mama trusts me. It is a blessed thing for a groom to know the family he is marrying into loves him as their own. And we should be joyful."

"I will not promise to be an obedient dutiful wife. No, not me - for I am a handsome, dashing fellow."

Amy pulls out a handkerchief and hands it to Nessie.

Nessie wipes her face, sniffing. "Percy, you're not humiliated that men come asking for money on the eve of your wedding?"

Amy shrugs. "Well, it has never happened to me before. I've lived a simple life on my farm – so much land, tending to so many sheep, content in my big, beautiful home, which is soon to be your home. So I don't know how to react except to be grateful. Today you will become my wife. We will dance and sing. There never was a happier man than I, to wed a beautiful, clever woman who waited a long, long time for me to come along. A kind woman, who believes in her fiancé – soon to be husband."

"Oh Percy, I was so worried …" Nessie melts. "But you are right. We will be happy. Won't we? I can't wait to be in your big, beautiful home. You think I'm beautiful?"

Her groom nods, then kisses her on the cheek. "Go and fix your lovely hair. I'll see you downstairs for our ceremony.

And then you will be Mrs Percival Carol Redwood."

After Nessie leaves, Amy makes certain her door is locked. She dashes to the bedside table and pulls out the ship tickets for their honeymoon – her getaway. She folds up the paperwork applying for mortgages, loans and life insurance, counts out the bills of the loans she has already received.

Next, Amy reaches for a small box on top of the cupboard. She opens it to marvel at the bracelets, necklaces and earrings, a collection of jewellery worth £114, all bought on credit through Nessie's brother-in-law.

The value of this one box is more than Amy could earn in a year as a teacher.

She hides her treasures in her bag, reminding herself: "Get through the wedding, then one more day, then I am out of here – the charming Percy Redwood will retire back into my imagination."

At the appointed hour, Amy swings on her jacket and goes downstairs to the large drawing room. The room is packed with flowers. The family guests, Nessie's mother, brothers and not one but two reverends all stand waiting.

People murmur about the groom.
"The nephew of the Archbishop."
"A champion horse rider."
"So generous – Percy gave all the bridesmaids gold necklaces!"
"Owns a run with 300 sheep."

There are darker whisperings too, but they are quickly shushed.

Amy, grinning, turns on the Percy charm, complimenting people, asking about their ailments, promising gifts and organising social events for after the honeymoon.

All the chatter ends as the piano starts to play.

The grand doors open. Eight flower girls enter, wearing white fluffy dresses with big blue bows, all purchased by Percy Redwood on credit. Next come the bridesmaids, followed at last by the bride with her father.

Everyone clusters around the older reverend, who speaks in booming tones.

The youngest flower girl peeps up at the groom, whispering in her quietest voice, "That man is a lady."

Only Amy hears the little girl. She winks at the child.

The reverend thunders on. "Does Nessie Otway take Percival Carol Redwood as her loving husband?"

Nessie, after a long pause, answers: "I do."

Amy quietly exhales with relief.

The newly married couple, now known as Nessie and Percy Redwood, step out on to the verandah, welcomed by the crowd of cheering guests throwing confetti into the bright sky.

Arm in arm with Nessie, from this vantage point high on the hill, Amy can see across the blue-water bay all the way to the lighthouse on the headland.

The newlyweds walk out into the garden to a grand marquee on the grounds of Nessie's parents' home. Inside great potted palms, long tables decked with food and multi-coloured flags bring a festive mood to the wedding party.

As the couple passes into the marquee, a pile of presents makes the groom's eyes light up. She especially likes the silver-mounted walking stick.

Amy laughs, moving about the marquee to receive congratulations and clink champagne glasses.

There are awkward moments.

She is stopped: "Mr Redwood, my dear fellow, you still owe me for the suit you are wearing."

"And there is no better tailor in this country than you," is the smooth reply. "Thank you for making me scrub up so handsome today. You've quite transformed me. There are many who would not recognise me as such an elegant gentleman. As soon as I have said hello to all my guests, I will duck upstairs and write you out a cheque. Your bill will be paid before you leave."

Another guest calls across the marquee. "Percy, Percy, thank you for the bike! Incredibly generous!"

Amy hurries over to shush him, not wanting the person she stole it from to hear.

And then one asks, "Your brother was meant to be best man, but he's not here! Nor your sister? Where's your mother?"

"I miss them terribly," says Amy. "But by chance my other sister is being married today, to a champion fellow about to depart for America. So her wedding is the more urgent. My family will visit in two short weeks, after our honeymoon."

The speeches provide a break from tricky questions. The local

member of parliament graciously wishes the newlyweds a bright future.

The sun sets on this perfect autumn day, glowing lanterns hang in the garden trees. Percy sits at the piano to play with the band, cheering on the dancers.

There is general agreement among the party, no dishonest soul could be so much fun. But from the piano stool, Amy sees some serious conversations with the father of the bride. Her new wife avoids her now.

Amy plays more merrily, calling for more champagne. At midnight, the groom is dancing, the last person on the dance floor. The band is exhausted.

The bride has already retired to bed, so Amy shares a bedroom with the best man. But she isn't about to give away her disguise. She collapses into bed in her fine wedding suit and is soon snoring soundly.

Early next morning, Amy's father-in-law stops her on the way to breakfast. "Percy, no father feels confident marrying his daughter off to a chap who has debts all over town. Until you pay up – she will be your wife in name only."

Amy nods. "Of course, Mr Ottaway, such generosity and wisdom. When my mother arrives with the money from the farm all will be cleared up. Do tell Nessie not to worry."

After a generous plate of eggs and chats with the remaining visitors, Amy sits to write thank-you cards to all the guests. At the same time, she calculates the value and transportability of their gifts.

"Hello, Amy," interrupts a softly spoken man, Police Detective Hunt. He sits on the chair beside her. "The game is up. Mr Percy Redwood – you are Miss Amy Bock, otherwise known as Mary Shannon, Amy Chanel, Agnes Vallance,

Charlotte Skevington and even Lady Balfour. I arrest you on charges of false means and fraud."

Amy winces. "Oh well. I guess I will have to tell you all about it. It's quite a yarn. If you have to do anything I'd appreciate you do it as quietly as possible, so as not to disturb the house."

"No, Amy – not this fraud. I've been chasing you about another case – you selling off all of one Mr John Roy's furniture while the poor man was away on holiday!"

As the police lead Mr Percy Redwood to their waiting buggy, Nessie runs out of the house.

"Percy Redwood, how could you?" she shouts. "How could you! You are not who you promised – you're not even a man! Poor me. I truly loved you!"

Amy turns and speaks quietly. "Loved me? No. You loved that I was whatever you wanted me to be, that I said what you wanted to hear, that I saw you the way you want to be seen. Remember, if something seems too good to be true, it probably is."

Amy Bock's impersonation landed her in jail for the defrauding of the Ottaways and their friends. She was also deemed a habitual criminal for her past cons. This con job was her last – the fame she earned from this incident forced her to stay within the bounds of the law (more or less) after her release from prison.

Grace

THE NEGOTIATING OUTLAW

More than 400 years ago, the English fought to conquer and control Ireland. Grace O'Malley, an Irish pirate, led her clan in rebellion, robbing ships in the northern seas and resisting English attacks. Her defiance of the English came at a great cost to her family ...

Grace shudders as she glances up at the gibbets – cages holding the remains of pirates, bandits and other sorry criminals. Ragged remnants of clothes flutter in the breeze.

Black birds perch on top of the cage bars, preening their feathers in the sunshine. The birds don't care that each gibbet marks the end of a life of adventure, of hopes and of hatreds.

The gibbets are grim landmarks dotted along the River Thames. Grace stares up at each cage from the rowboat she is travelling in. She is being taken to the Queen of England's summer residence, Greenwich Castle.

For Grace, each cage sharpens her understanding of the Queen of England. Elizabeth the First is a ruthless ruler.

Grace thinks of her sons. It makes her feel braver. "This is my last gamble to save my boys. I won't leave them prisoners of the English governor Richard Bingham. I will not rest while Bingham says he will execute my sons. Maybe I am being rowed into a trap, but I am no captive. I demanded this meeting with the English queen."

Grace smiles to herself. "No gibbets can scare me off for I am also a queen – Grace, Queen of Pirates."

From a bend in the river Grace first glimpses her destination. As she is rowed into the pier, she gazes at the sprawling castle. Its famous red bricks are bright against the blue sky. It is different to Grace's fortress far away in the north, with its massive squares of dark grey rock. Greenwich Castle's gardens roll graciously down to the river. Grace's fortress has no garden – the whole place is barely the size of one of these towers. She counts this castle's many windows. Her own has only one on each side, on the top floor, so she can see her enemies coming. Grace's fortress is accessible only at high tide, making it almost impossible to attack. It has one function: to protect her and her family. This castle is positioned perfectly to flaunt power and wealth.

Grace makes a calculation in her head as her boat is tied to the pier. "This fancy, show-off castle is poorly defended. I would not need many pirates to storm it."

A welcoming party of courtiers strain to see Grace's arrival. They rush forward along the pier. But before anyone can offer assistance, Grace stands and springs from the boat. She has lived most of her sixty years on ships. Age has not robbed her of balance or strength.

As the courtiers lead her to their queen, Grace notes the golden corridors, the tapestries and the multitudes of men and women in silks and velvets. This is the luxury she has heard of, so she is not awed by it. Rather she strides down the corridors, heading boldly towards the throne room.

At its entrance, the guards open the huge wooden doors. At the far end of the room, Queen Elizabeth sits in splendour on her throne.

Grace hears the gasps, the shocked muttering and nervous exclamations of the royal court:
"How brutish!"
"She's a pirate!"
"A barbarian!"

Grace keeps walking until she is at the steps of the magnificent throne.

"You forgot to bow," Queen Elizabeth says in a droll tone.

"Ah, no," quips Grace with a smile. "One sovereign does not bow to another, and I am queen of my people."

Surprisingly, Elizabeth grins back at her. "Funny. I heard you were queen of the murderers, bandits and pirates."

"Well, them too," answers Grace. "But of course not Sir Francis Drake – he's your pirate."

Elizabeth laughs, but not with the usual simper that hides her rotten teeth. Instead it is a real, hearty laugh. "Don't let the Spanish ambassador hear you say that. My pirates are strictly privateers …"

"And any gold they bring you is only a fair and just tax," finishes Grace.

"Exactly!" says Elizabeth.

The two women observe each other keenly. They are the same age, past the time of bearing children, but otherwise completely different.

Grace stands in a long, dark green gown with a brilliant green silk cloak. Her grey hair is pulled back into a bun. Across her forehead stretches a deep scar, torn by the talons of an eagle she fought when she was just a child.

Elizabeth's wrinkles and smallpox scars are concealed by thick layers of make-up, and a brilliant red wig covers her thinning hair. The jewels sewn onto her dress represent the vast wealth of her kingdom.

Grace interrupts the silence. "I have sailed a long way to talk with you."

"Let's talk properly then," says Elizabeth. "We shall sit by the fire. It may be summer but this room is always cold."

Queen Elizabeth rises from the throne.

Two guards step forward to search Grace for weapons. Grace pulls out a long silver dagger. The men draw their swords in alarm.

Elizabeth watches on, raising one very plucked eyebrow in disapproval.

Grace shrugs. "You wouldn't expect me to come unarmed to the castle of those who killed one of my sons and arrested the others?"

"There is reason in your statement," acknowledges Elizabeth. "But daggers will not be necessary. My guards will mind your weapon but respect your safety."

Grace thinks of her mission and bravely hands over her blade.

> "My sons, your Majesty. This is why I have come to you."

The women retire to glorious chairs by the fire.

Elizabeth shoos back her courtiers. "We will talk in private."

At Elizabeth's invitation Grace begins: "My sons, your Majesty. This is why I have come to you. Your governor, Bingham, is a vicious man. He is about to try my two surviving boys and my half-brother for treason.
The trial will not be fair. He means to execute them."

"Yes, Governor Bingham writes to me. You and your clan

constantly plunder his boats, attack his soldiers, then disappear into the forest, wage war on him …"

"Does he tell you he attacks us with huge armies – 25 English soldiers to each one of my clan – and that he burns our lands so our people starve? And that he killed my eldest son without trial?"

Elizabeth is silent.

"Starving people will fight – they have nothing to lose," says Grace. "Your governor offers us slow death from misery or the fast death of revolt. Your governor makes you a tyrant. In my battle with him I have already lost one son. If you return the others to me, I'll not fight you or yours. No treasure can compare to the treasure of my boys."

Still Elizabeth says nothing.

Grace pushes on: "It is better to have a pirate like me on your side rather than against you. Give me back my sons."

Elizabeth replies thoughtfully. "Yes, a son would be a great treasure."

On the other side of the room, the courtiers watch the two leaders draw closer to talk of precious things, their struggles, the rareness of their kind.

As the fire dies and the sun dips beneath the windows, Grace stands.

She bows to Queen Elizabeth. Their conversation is finished.

After this meeting, Grace returned to her fortress at Clew Bay. Her sons were released from prison, she was pardoned of all alleged crimes and her lands were recognised by royal decree. Governor Bingham was called back to England to answer the charges Grace had made against him. This was a small pause in the conflict, for the English continued their war on the Irish and the Irish continued to resist. But the famous pirate Grace O'Malley died peacefully in her own bed – the same year as Queen Elizabeth.

Martina

THE REDEMPTIVE OUTLAW

About 200 years ago, Martina Chapanay was the daughter of an indigenous Huarpe chief. It was a time when there was a renewed push to steal the lands of indigenous people in Argentina, and the country was torn by a series of civil wars. Martina fought with paramilitary groups and formal militias, but she also took control of a group of bandits.

Martina stretches out on the bleached sand. Her head rests on her folded poncho. Her hat tilts down over her eyes. She's not asleep. Her boots are on. The reins of her horse wrap loosely around her hand. Martina is listening intently.

The other bandits in her gang sit on the slope. They are restless but know to keep quiet. Their horses stand awkwardly, heads down, occasionally swishing their tails in the heat.

All of them hear the distant turn of wheels rolling, coming closer, on the road above them. The horses look up.

One of the bandits coughs nervously to get Martina's attention.

"Bah," she snorts. "I'm not getting up to rob some poor farmer. What would we get? A donkey? It's hard to share a donkey between twelve bandits."

The bandit groans and fans his hat over his face. "But we've been here since before dawn. This drought means we need something … anything."

"We steal from the caudillo," Martina reminds him. "Only those military big men and politicians carry enough gold to risk our lives for."

"That drunk soldier, he bragged that the big pay day is today. But maybe he made a mistake," replies the bandit. "He was very drunk! Maybe he doesn't even work for the caudillo. Maybe they aren't coming. Maybe they took a different road!"

Martina adjusts her hat but doesn't bother to reply.

"Martina," pleads the bandit. "You don't feel the heat or the cold."

"Yes, I do," she corrects him. "I just don't complain."

The bandit doesn't give up. "This caudillo is a rich man. He will have his own militia with him, his own men. Loyal to him."

"I've been militia," grunts Martina. "I know militia. There's more of us than them, and we have the advantage of surprise. No one expects the caudillo to be attacked on land he thinks he owns, especially the caudillo himself."

The bandit repeatedly stabs his facón, his favourite knife with its large heavy blade, into the sand.

"Only those military big men and politicians carry enough gold to risk our lives for."

Martina mutters, "Waiting makes you nervous. Clean your guns or sleep, dream about the gold you're gonna pocket. I'll wake you up when it is time."

The sun moves across the sky, the shadow retreats across the sand.

Martina lifts the brim of her hat. "Now we're gonna have to move. No shadow in this ravine – we'll be visible for miles around."

As she rises on to her knees, Martina hears what she's been listening for: horses galloping full pelt, lots of horses, and a carriage with wheels spinning.

She clicks her fingers at her crew. She motions to four riders. They understand her hand signals and disappear into the sandy crevasses, leading away from the road.

The other bandits follow Martina. She scrambles up the ridge, leading her horse back up on to the road. The carriage comes closer and closer.

Martina jumps up onto her horse. Her team assembles in formation behind her.

As the last bandit scrambles into his saddle, the first of the militia round the corner. Martina greets them astride her horse, in the middle of the road with her long flintlock rifle pointed straight at them. Behind her, two bandits fire into the air. Bang! Bang!

The oncoming horses rear up. More militia round the corner, wrenching their horses to the side, trying to prevent collision.

Martina nods. Chaos explodes! Men! Horses! Shouting! Shooting! Dust!

Too much action for this confined corner. The road drops away down the steep sand banks on one side. The rock wall rises up on the other side. There is nowhere for the animals and their riders to go.

As the carriage rounds into the corner, it skids to a sharp halt.

A man, in a fine military uniform, pokes his head out of the carriage. "Idiots! Back up! Shoot! Attack! Kill those bandits!! Back up! GET ME OUT OF HERE!!!"

The rest of Martina's bandits gallop up behind the carriage. There is no retreat for the caudillo. His convoy is surrounded by Martina's gang. One excited bandit climbs to the top of the carriage, jumps up and down, firing his guns at the sun, hollering at the militia below him.

Martina rides through the crowd to the carriage window. She signals quiet to the bandit hollering above. She slides out her facón, using the heavy blade to knock on the carriage window.

One of the militia, crowded near the carriage, pulls close to Martina. He draws his sword.

A shot rings out. The militia man drops his sword, falling off his horse before he can wound Martina. His sword is trampled under horse hooves.

LAWLESS LADIES | 84

The bandit on top of the carriage grins at Martina as he blows the top of his musket.

Martina ignores this attempt on her life, knocking again on the carriage window. She can see the man cowering inside, shrinking into his impressive blue jacket with gold-plated military lapels.

Martina orders him. "You need to pay us to pass this road."

"Money. I can give you money," agrees the man.

Martina shakes her head. "I won't take your paper money. That gets me something here, but nothing there. Or nothing here but something there. Or nothing anywhere. Gold has real value. You know it, because that is how you pay your men. I know it, because that is how I pay mine."

The cowering man now peers up at Martina. "You're a woman. Now I see it. I hear it in your voice. I'm not giving any gold to a woman. I've never done it before. I'm not doing it now."

"Yes you are," states Martina, wrenching the door open. "And I'm happy to give you this new experience."

Two of her bandits climb into the carriage. One pushes his gun into the fine wool of the fancy blue jacket.

The other bandit searches the carriage. Under the seats, he finds two heavy bags of gold. Cheering, the bandits jump down from the carriage, throwing the bags up to Martina.

Another bandit smashes one wheel of the carriage with an axe.

Martina shoots her gun in the air. All the bandits turn and gallop off, disappearing down the road, across the sand, into the old folds of the dry land.

That night, by the light of the campfire, Martina divides up the gold between her crew.

"Smile, boss!" shouts one of the happy bandits.

Martina shrugs. "There ain't a lot to smile about."

The men laugh at her melancholy. She isn't diverted from her task. For every piece that goes to her team, one piece is placed in the middle. The central pile grows larger and larger.

Martina takes the central pile of gold and sweeps it back into a bag. None of the men comment when she gets on her horse with her bag of gold and leaves the camp of celebrating bandits.

Martina rides across the dusty plain. Her first stop is a little hut, with some mangy goats and a thin cow fenced out the back. She knocks on the door.

A woman holding a crying baby barely cracks open the door. Martina holds out her hand with a piece of gold. The woman gasps, blesses Martina, takes the gold, then closes the door.

Martina rides on through the village, another hut, another door.

One old man peers out at her. "I know who you are. You are not just some guacho. Do you think we the poor people will protect you, we will risk ourselves for you? Are you buying my silence?"

Martina sighs. "No. I'm earning redemption."

With that she rides into the darkness.

Martina lived a long life: fighting for generals she believed in, earning herself at least one pardon because of her bravery, working as a tracker and famous as a bandit for just causes. When she returned to her home village she found desolation, with nobody left alive. She found refuge in an indigenous village in Mogna. She died in old age from the bite of a deadly animal – some say it was a snake, others say a puma.

Cheng I Sao

THE WISE OUTLAW

Cheng I Sao – also known as Ching Shih, Shi Xianggu, Madam Ching and Jehng Sih – was the most successful pirate of all time. More than 200 years ago, she commanded the largest fleet ever seen and enforced a strict code of conduct among her pirates that ensured discipline. Cheng I Sao also set up a protection system whereby merchants and fishermen paid her for the right to sail in the South China Sea.

Cheng I Sao slams down her bowl. The crash cuts through the clamour of pirates shouting with spittle-flecked rage, their fists and weapons raised. Her glare sucks all air from the room.

The Blue Flag Fleet commander shudders. The Green Fleet commander whimpers. The Black Fleet commander lowers his dagger. Even Cheng I Sao's husband, the Red Fleet commander, stops drinking his soup.

Their ever-calm leader has shocked them all with uncharacteristic fury.

While they tremble, Cheng I Sao assesses the men gathered at her table. Once they were keen and sharp, but they have grown bloated and arrogant.

Now her men scrap among themselves for more power and more trinkets.

All that can be heard is waves slapping against the side of the elegant ship from which she rules her pirate empire.

Cheng I Sao turns her eye on each man present. They know her strict code of conduct: if you break a single rule, your head is chopped off and your body thrown into the sea.

She finally speaks, her voice a menacing whisper. "I will not have this fighting, this constant betrayal of each other. We are the confederation. We rule these seas. Ten years ago we were nothing more than a rabble of pirates. Now we are organised, united and stronger than any navy or army. But if you all persist in this short-sighted behaviour, stealing from each other, then we won't control a cleaning cloth. We are only as strong as our loyalty to each other. Greed will sink us all."

That night in her chamber, Cheng I Sao paces the floor. Her long black hair swishes back and forth as she walks. The room is small, as are all rooms on ships, but this one is a jewel box, inset with beautiful wood carvings and mother-of-pearl.

From the bed, her husband Chang Pao attempts to soothe her, "Dangerous as you are, you're no shark. You must stop moving to sleep. Come to bed."

But Cheng I Sao keeps pacing.

Again her husband tries to lure her to bed, "You're the terror of the South China Sea. You command 70,000 men. We've more than one thousand boats. We're unbeatable! We're making more money than ever before. Now every merchant and fisherman pays us for protection. We're the pirates and the navy combined, we're the enforcers and the thieves! You have nothing to worry about – on water, you are everything!"

"Don't be a fool. We're at the top of the wave now, but the sea rolls on." Cheng I Sao continues back and forth against the rhythm of the ship.

"I don't understand this at all," says Chang Pao, pulling his blanket up to his chin. "I thought we were doing well, for a poor fisherman and a girl who started life with nothing – no land, no family, no friends." He chuckles. "So poor, she was raised on water."

His wife explains, "Now we are powerful because you command the Red Flag Fleet. It is still the largest fleet, and we have rules and deals that mean we have the allegiance of the others. But they are not truly loyal to us."

"You pay them to be loyal. You pay them a lot!" he retorts.

"They all want more. Greedy, greedy, greedy. My dear husband, the captain of the Black Flag Fleet openly talks about killing you."

"Ahh, that is because he is jealous. He loves you and wants to be your husband," chuckles Chang Pao.

"Love. Ha! None of us know love. He wants to be captain of your fleet."

Her husband scratches at his beard. "Maybe you should just cut off his head and feed his body to the fish?"

Cheng I Sao raises her eyebrows. "Our problem is not with one – it's with all of them. We have too many commanders, too many men. We are too big. The reward is immense for anyone who overthrows us. It is time to change."

Then, more softly, she asks, "Think, my husband, how do pirates usually finish?"

He grumbles with his eyes shut: "As fish food, blown away by cannons or hanging at the end of the noose."

"Yes, and we are not going to suffer any of those endings. It is time we surrendered to the Governor of Guangzhou!"

"What? Surrender?" Chang Pao's eyes pop open, suddenly wide awake. "Now you're mad! He will hang us before you can say 'good morning'!"

"No. You will go and negotiate a settlement, while we are strong. We will build a new life."

With that, Cheng I Sao stops pacing, blows out her lamp and slips into bed. She rolls over and goes to sleep, leaving her husband awake to worry about meeting the governor.

At the next gathering of commanders, Cheng I Sao gets straight to the point. "It is my most fervent wish that you all escape the horrible deaths common to pirates and live to be old men."

This statement captures the commanders' attention.

Cheng I Sao continues. "A few days ago my husband tried to strike an armistice with the Governor of Guangzhou so that we may all take the treasure we've won and retire from this life of piracy, to start afresh on land."

Cheng I Sao sighs. "Unfortunately, the governor is a foolish man, and sent a foolish envoy who foolishly would not give my husband what we want. Therefore I must go directly to the governor. For this mission I don't need you lot. I need your wives and daughters. The commander of every fleet – all of you – must deliver me your wives and daughters."

"My wife?" challenges the Green Flag Fleet commander.

Cheng I Sao clenches her teeth. Everyone notes the firming of her jaw.

The commanders do not understand, but they obey.

"I am here to end piracy and therefore must speak to the governor."

With her assembly of women and girls, Cheng I Sao is ready. She sails her ships straight to Guangzhou. The harbour is crowded with ships – from small sampans to large junks – fishermen, floating stores, family homes, merchants, shops, gambling houses. It is a whole other city on the water.

The pirate ships glide through this water maze. Cheng I Sao breathes in the salty tang of sea air mixed with the smoke of hundreds of cooking fires, the smells of her childhood.

At the pier she disembarks, leading her delegation of women

and girls, gloriously dressed in red silk waving in the wind. Not one of them carries a weapon.

The delegation makes its way up the widest avenue, away from the crowded lanes of the port, past the huge warehouses of the foreign traders, up to the gates of the official headquarters.

Curious people follow.

The crowd strains to hear as Cheng I Sao announces at the gate: "I am here to end piracy and therefore must speak to the governor."

The soldiers at the gate stand back and allow the red wave of female pirates to pass.

Cheng I Sao leads the women and girls to the main hall, where yellow and black silk curtains hang from the ceiling, all the way down to the mats across the floor.

Warned of this remarkable delegation, the governor stands waiting behind a long wooden table in his dark silk robes, with a high cream collar and his official black hat. He is flanked by his assistants, and officials and merchants sit on benches lining the walls. All are fascinated to see the legendary Cheng I Sao, the pirate who has intimidated them for the last ten years.

She bows low. Her women and the girls do the same.

"Oh most honourable and knowledgeable Governor, he who guides the people of Guangzhou with wisdom and compassion, I am the humble Cheng I Sao. I am here to offer you the end of piracy in the South China Sea, to free you from the scourge of thieves and restore the rightful balance to the waters of this great and glorious empire."

This elaborate, respectful speech confuses the governor. He

expects a rough pirate, not this calm woman. "The end of thieves and who? What balance? The end of p-pira-piracy?" he splutters.

"All of the pirates of the confederation will surrender. You can report to the emperor that you ended Cheng I Sao's reign of terror." Cheng I Sao gestures towards the governor. "A hero. This will be the largest retirement of thieves ever. The end of criminality."

The merchants and officials murmur approvingly.

"These are my conditions," Cheng I Sao proclaims. "I tell you publicly so all can hear what I promise and know I am true to my word. First, I will be known as Lady of Imperial Rank Cheng I Sao, recognised as nobility, so nobody can charge me for what has happened in the past. Second, I, and all my pirates, will be paid to return to the land, so we have money to start a new life."

Here the governor coughs, realising he is being fitted with an enormous bill for the retirement of thousands of pirates. "What about all the goods, the gold, the money you have stolen?"

Cheng I Sao sighs theatrically. "It is expensive being a pirate, every boat consumes thousands of pounds of fruit, vegetables, rice, pork – a whole cow every two or three days! And we now have nothing left."

Some in the grand hall stifle their laughter. How can a woman in such a glorious gown say she has nothing?

"Third, my husband will be given an officer's rank in the army and allowed to keep thirty boats to continue his salt trading."

The governor slams his fist on the table. "No! No! No! Are you mad? No punishment for your years of crime? For those killed? Those terrorised? Why should I do anything for a bunch of women and girls?" he shouts.

"Because we come peacefully, without weapons, as a sign of respect. Because we represent the largest pirate fleet in the world. And if I do not return to my ship with our demands met, then my pirate commanders, the husbands of these women, will sail straight to this city. These men have never feared death at the bottom of the sea. They do not fear you or your punishments. They will burn your city to the ground." Cheng I Sao pauses.

"All foreign trade through our glorious empire will be reduced to ash," she continues. "We women and girls, we offer you a new future – a future free of pirates."

The merchants and officials turn to look at the governor.

The governor gazes at the woman before him. She has already defeated his navy, the Portuguese and the British. He can think of no way to refuse.

He bows to her. "Lady of Imperial Rank Cheng I Sao."

Cheng I Sao moved ashore and opened a massive gambling house. Her husband had a successful military career serving the Emperor while she continued to grow her fortune and lived to an old age.